HITLER'S ENFORCERS